INSIDE A
TRAIN

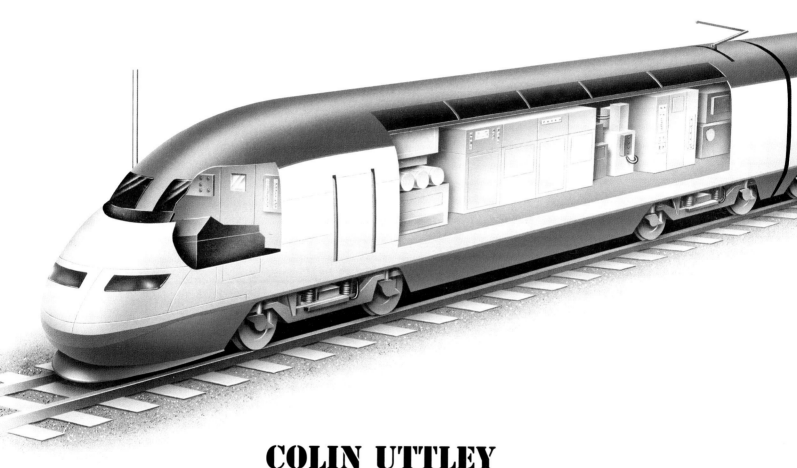

COLIN UTTLEY

angus

This edition published in 2004
by Angus Books Ltd
12 Ravensbury Terrace
London SW18 4RL

ISBN 1-904594-51-4

FOR BROWN PARTWORKS
Project editor: Roland Hill
Consultant: Dr. Derek Smith
Designer: Sarah Williams
Illustrator:Matthew White (main artwork), Mark Walker
Managing editor: Anne O'Daly
Picture researcher: Sean Hannaway

Production by Omnipress,
Eastbourne, UK
Printed and bound in Dubai

Contents

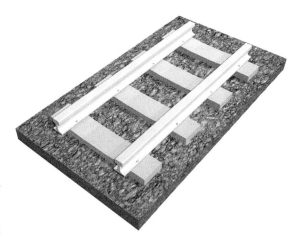

History 4

Inside a train 6

High-speed problems 8

Construction and materials 10

Power 12

In the driver's and passenger's seat 14

Signalling 16

Cutting through the air 18

Full stop 20

On the tracks 22

Suspension 24

Through and over 26

The future 28

Glossary 30

Index 32

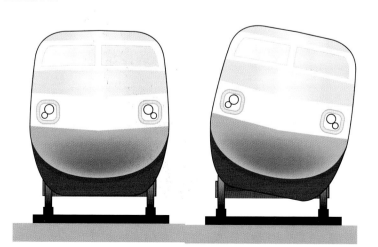

History

People have always wanted to travel faster and to save time travelling. Trains are one of the oldest forms of public mass-transport and have developed greatly since 1825, when the first public railroad opened.

That first railway was in England. High-speed trains did not start to develop until the 1930s, when designers looked at ways of making their steam trains travel faster. They built trains that cut through the air more easily than anything that had gone before. These trains were called streamliners. The fastest was *Mallard*.

Until World War II the fastest trains were steam trains. After the war electric and diesel trains were developed. This is *Mallard*.

In 1938 *Mallard*, a British train, reached a speed of 126 miles per hour (202km/h) while pulling four carriages. This is the fastest that a steam train has ever travelled.

In 1955 the French railways made high-speed experiments using two of their latest electric locomotives on a straight piece of track. On March 28 the locomotive CC7107 reached a new world record speed of 205.7 miles per hour (331km/h). The next day another French locomotive, BB9004, matched that speed exactly.

The record-breaking French locomotive CC7107. It had a very square front, unlike modern trains.

Bullet trains

In the late 1950s Japan's railway system was in a mess. It was overcrowded and outdated—something had to be done. The answer was to build a completely new line for the latest high-speed electric trains. When it opened in 1964, the new system, called the Shinkansen (meaning "new main line" in Japanese), was the most modern in the world. Its sleek trains travelled at 130 miles per hour (209km/h) and became famous around the world as bullet trains.

The TGV (Train à Grand Vitesse). These colourful trains are found all over Europe. This one travels from Paris to Lyon in France.

The fastest high-speed trains

The French TGV (Train à Grand Vitesse, which means high-speed train) is the fastest train in the world today. It usually cruises at 186 miles per hour (299km/h). In 1990 a TGV was tested to find out just how fast it could go. The result was a world record 320.3 miles per hour (515km/h).

The German high-speed train is called the ICE (Inter-City Express) and it travels around Germany and Switzerland at speeds up to 186 miles per hour (299km/h). The newest version, ICE-3, does not have a separate power car; each of the carriages supplies some of the power to drive the train.

The Acela Express speeds between Washington, D.C., and Boston, Mass., at a top speed of 165 miles per hour (266km/h). It is the latest and fastest train in the U.S. The carriages of the Acela Express are designed to tilt as they take the many sharp curves between Washington and Boston. This makes the long journey much more comfortable for passengers.

Inside a train

High-speed trains are not the same as other, slower trains. High-speed trains need to be built from special materials, and they need to travel on carefully maintained high-speed tracks.

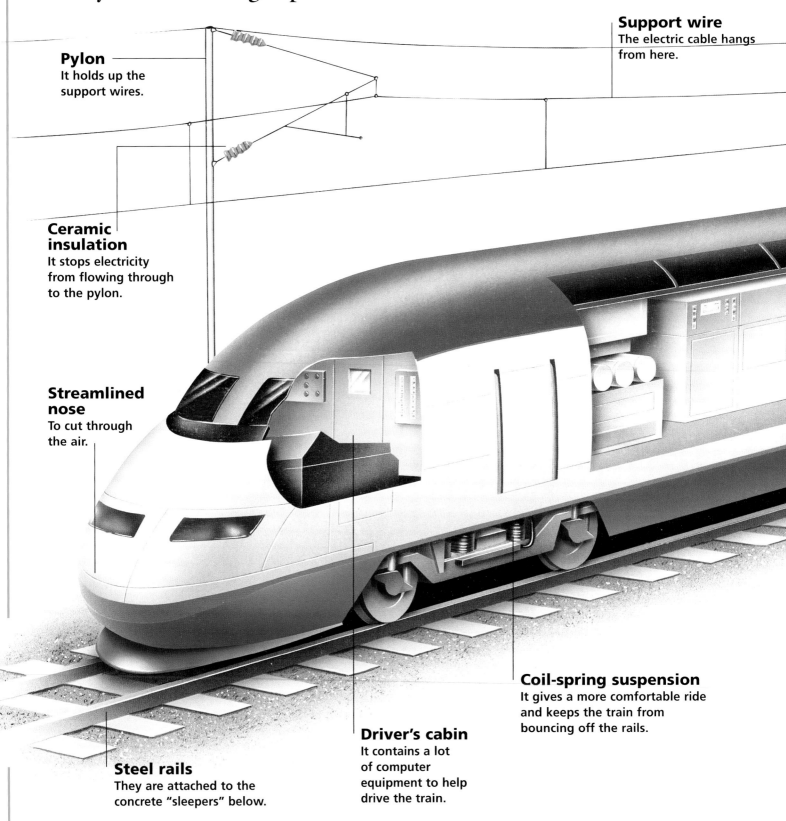

Support wire
The electric cable hangs from here.

Pylon
It holds up the support wires.

Ceramic insulation
It stops electricity from flowing through to the pylon.

Streamlined nose
To cut through the air.

Coil-spring suspension
It gives a more comfortable ride and keeps the train from bouncing off the rails.

Driver's cabin
It contains a lot of computer equipment to help drive the train.

Steel rails
They are attached to the concrete "sleepers" below.

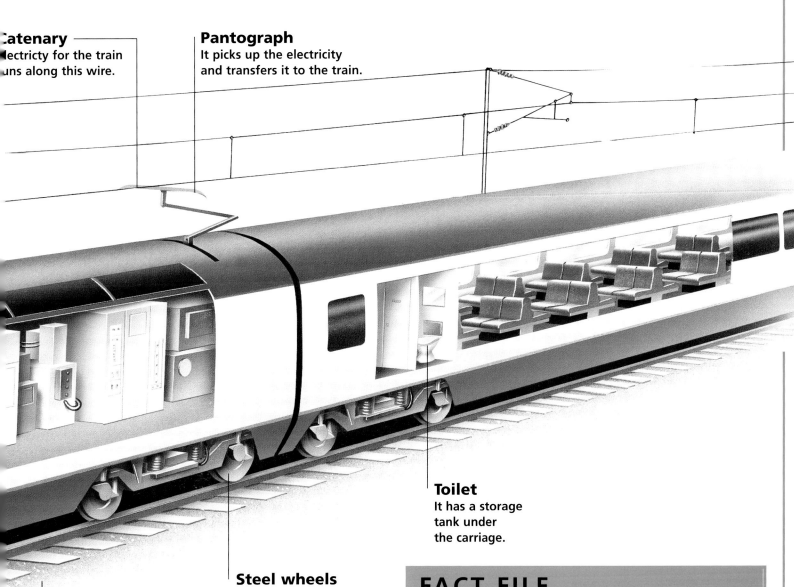

Catenary
Electricty for the train runs along this wire.

Pantograph
It picks up the electricity and transfers it to the train.

Toilet
It has a storage tank under the carriage.

Steel wheels
They are very strong.

Ballast
This coarse gravel under the tracks is thicker than for slow-speed lines.

FACT FILE

⭘ The TGV is the most popular high-speed train. It has been exported to many countries. In Belgium and Germany it is called Thalys, in Spain it is called AVE (Alta Velocidad Española), in England it is called Eurostar, and in South Korea it is called KTX.

⭘ You can see the headlights on Japanese Shinkansen (bullet trains) from 1.6 miles (2km) away, even in daylight.

High-speed problems

One of the reasons that old-fashioned railways are slow is that they have lots of sharp bends. Trains have to slow down so that they can take the bends safely. New high-speed railroads are built with as few curves as possible so that trains do not have to slow down.

When a high-speed railway has to go through hilly countryside, the trains are powerful enough to take the gradients (slopes) at high speed, and unlike bends, there is no need to slow down for a hill. The extra energy that the train needs to get up the hill is saved coming down the other side.

When a high-speed train goes into a tunnel, air is compressed (squashed) between the train and the tunnel walls. This air will flow very quickly into the inside of the train if there are any openings for it to go through. If the air pressure hits the passengers' ears, it

can be very painful. To stop this from happening, the air vents and other openings on a high-speed train are automatically closed as the train enters a tunnel. They are only opened again when the train comes out of the other end of the tunnel.

High-speed trains push the air around them aside very quickly as they travel. When two trains pass each other going in opposite directions, the blast of air from both trains is

This German ICE-1 train is running on track built to be used only by high-speed trains.

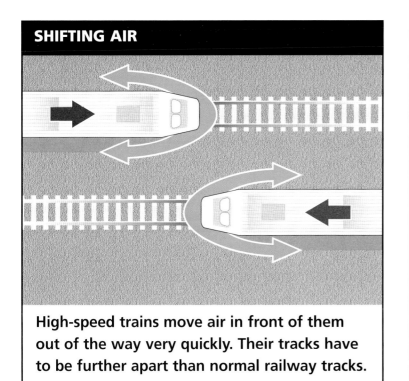

High-speed trains move air in front of them out of the way very quickly. Their tracks have to be further apart than normal railway tracks.

FACT FILE

◯ If high-speed trains pass each other many times in a tunnel, eventually the air pressure can be strong enough to break the windows.

◯ A high-speed train takes 3.3 miles (5.3km) to stop when travelling at 168 mph (270km/h).

◯ Think about the hills, rivers, and buildings in your neighbourhood. Where would you put a high-speed railway?

◯ Next time you are at a railway station, listen to the sound of trains passing at different speeds.

squashed between them. On a normal railway this blast of air could be strong enough to topple the trains from the track. On high-speed railways the tracks are built much farther apart than other railways.

This gives enough room for trains to pass each other safely. High-speed trains make a lot of noise as they move. On many new lines walls are built next to the track so that people living nearby are less disturbed.

Construction and materials

High-speed trains are designed to be as light as possible. Weight can be saved by using the right materials and by the way the trains are built.

Most trains are built of steel. This strong metal is rolled between powerful rollers to make thin sheets. The sheets are cut and folded into the right shape. Different sections of the train can then be joined together by welding. Sometimes a flame is used to melt the two pieces of metal together.

A factory where high-speed trains are put together. The train on the left is nearly finished.

Another type of welding uses a powerful electric current flowing across two pieces of metal to melt them together. It is called arc welding. Some trains are made from aluminium, a metal that is much lighter than steel. Aluminium does not rust, so the trains can save even more weight because they do not have to be painted.

Building a train

Carriages used to be built in two parts. A heavy, flat metal frame called a chassis gave the carriage most of its strength. The carriage's body was fastened to the top of the chassis, and the bogies, with the suspension and wheels, were fastened under it. Today the bogies are fastened directly to the underneath of the carriage. There is no separate chassis, so the whole train is lighter.

The windows of a high-speed train must be very strong, but at the same time it must be possible to break through them so passengers can escape if there is an emergency. Most of the central part of the window is made from laminated glass. It is made by sandwiching a layer of plastic between two sheets of glass. Laminated glass is very strong and does not shatter if something hits it. Sometimes the windows have an outer and inner layer separated by a gap filled with air.

The corners of the window are made from toughened glass. Although it is strong, this type of glass will break if it is hit hard enough. If the train has an accident and people are trapped inside, rescue teams can break the windows by hitting the corners with a hammer, and passengers can escape.

FACT FILE

◐ A 16-car train made of aluminium will weigh approximately 211 tonnes (215t) less than the same sized train made of steel.

◐ The driver's window in a high-speed train is made of toughened, or laminated, glass approximately one inch (25mm) thick.

◐ Next time you are on a train, try to work out what the different parts of the train are made of and how they are put together. Look out for the parts of the window that are designed to be broken in an emergency.

This man is putting parts of a train carriage together by welding. He is wearing a mask to avoid damaging his eyes in the bright light.

Power

Most high-speed trains are driven by electric motors. Often two parts of the train are equipped with motors. They are called the power cars and are usually put at the front and the back of the train.

Sometimes the motors in a train are fixed to the axle next to the wheels, but in most high-speed trains they are inside the power cars. Metal shafts join motors to the wheels.

Electric motors have a steel rod called a spindle that runs through the middle of their rotor. Around the spindle long lengths of wire are tightly coiled together and wedged into an iron core. Electromagnets are positioned close to, but not quite touching, the rotor. When electricity flows through the wire, it makes the wire magnetic—it acts like a magnet. The rotor magnet and the stationary magnet close to it try to move relative to each other, and the motor turns. As long as electricity is flowing through the wire, the motor will try to turn. When the electricity is cut off, the wire stops being magnetic, and the motor stops driving.

Power up

The electricity needed to turn the motors is carried along wires hanging from pylons above the railway line. These wires are called the catenary. The electricity in the catenary is picked up by a device on the top of the train called a pantograph. Pantographs have a strip of metal at their top that rubs against the wires of the catenary. Electricity flows from the catenary, down the pantograph, and into the motors. The pantograph must just touch the wires. If it pushes too hard against them, the pantograph and the wires will wear away quickly. If it does not touch strongly enough,

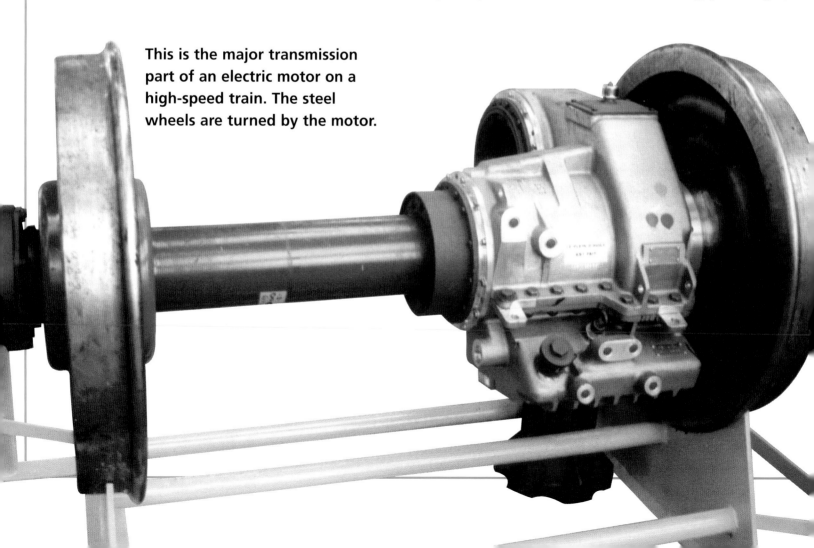

This is the major transmission part of an electric motor on a high-speed train. The steel wheels are turned by the motor.

MAKE AN ELECTROMAGNET

You will need a 1.5-volt battery, an iron bolt or nail, about 2 yards (2m) of glazed copper wire, 2 pieces of plain wire, adhesive tape, and scissors.

1 Wind the wire around the bolt or nail, keeping the coils close together. When you reach the end, put a small piece of tape on the wire and start to wind a second layer of wire over the first one, again keeping the coils close together.

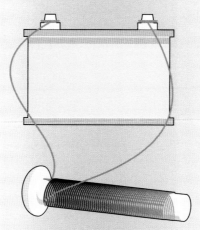

3 When the two ends are attached to the battery, you can use your electromagnet to pick up small pins or nails. When the battery is disconnected, the electromagnet loses most of its power.

2 Attach a piece of plain wire to either end of the wire. Join the other ends to the battery.

Right: The pantograph (attached to the train) and the catenary (the wires that carry electricity).

the electricity will not flow properly.

The electric motors of some trains do not get their power from overhead cables. Instead, they are equipped with their own generators that they carry with them. Sometimes diesel motors are used to drive an electric generator. An electric generator is very like an electric motor, but instead of putting electricity into it to make it turn, it does the opposite—when it is turned, it makes electricity. The diesel motor of a diesel-electric locomotive drives an electric generator, which makes electricity to turn the electric drive motors. Sometimes gas turbine engines like the ones in aeroplanes are used to drive the electric generator.

FACT FILE

◯ **Next time you make a train journey, look out for the catenary. If there isn't one, what do you think powers the trains?**

In the driver's and passenger's seat

The driver of a high-speed train must know what is happening to all parts of the train and that the track ahead is clear. The passengers should be comfortable and relaxed for their journey.

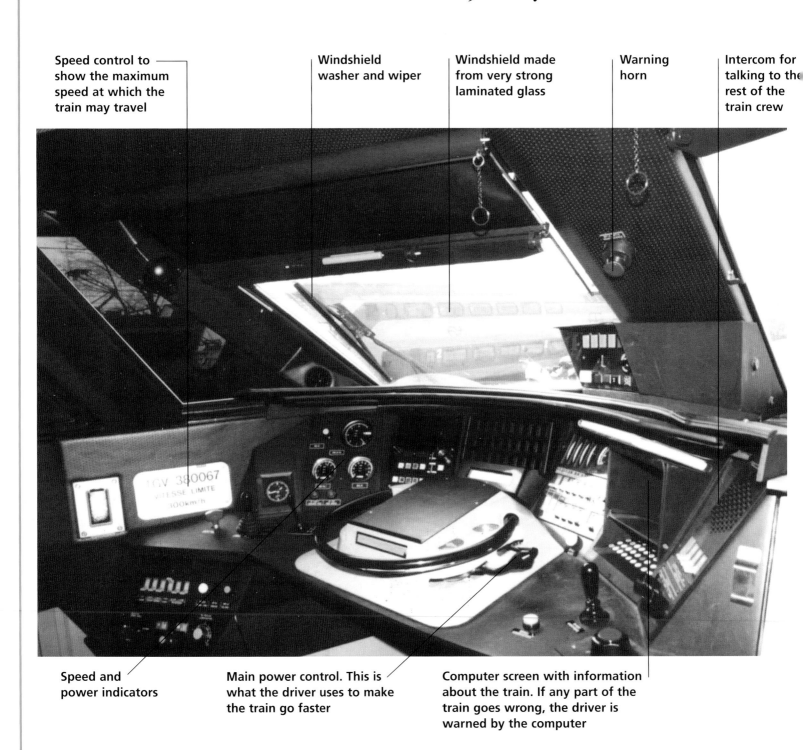

Speed control to show the maximum speed at which the train may travel

Windshield washer and wiper

Windshield made from very strong laminated glass

Warning horn

Intercom for talking to the rest of the train crew

Speed and power indicators

Main power control. This is what the driver uses to make the train go faster

Computer screen with information about the train. If any part of the train goes wrong, the driver is warned by the computer

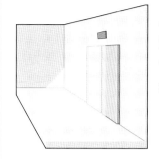

Drivers of high-speed trains are often shown how to drive trains by simulators. They look just like the control cabs of the real train, with all the same controls and equipment, but they stay inside a building. Everything a driver does in the real train can be tried out first in the simulator without any risk to the train or passengers.

The carriages of many high-speed trains are becoming more like airliners. Seats are equipped with personal stereos and flatscreen TVs. Buffet bars are being replaced by meals served directly to passengers at their seats.

| Ventilation and individual passenger lights | Carriage lighting | Automatic doors | Reclining seats. When a button is pressed, the seat tilts back to make the passenger more comfortable |

Signalling

Trains can only travel quickly if there is no danger of driving into the other trains on the line. Signalling is used to warn drivers of what is happening ahead of them on the line and to keep trains a safe distance apart.

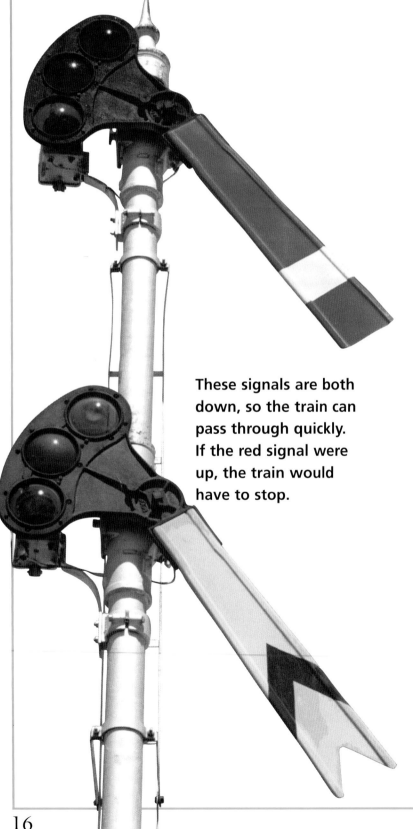

These signals are both down, so the train can pass through quickly. If the red signal were up, the train would have to stop.

Many railways still use coloured light signals at the side of the track. They are like the traffic lights used on roads. Usually red means stop, amber means caution, and green means that it is safe to go.

The type of signalling that has been used in most of the world for the last 130 years relies on electricity flowing through the railway lines. The railway is divided into lengths of about one mile (1.6km). These lengths are called blocks. Electricity flows up one rail; and when a train goes into the block, the electricity flows across the train's wheels to the other line. As soon as that happens, the system shows there is a train in that block. Only one train at a time is allowed into each block and the two neighbouring blocks, so trains are kept at least one block apart. This system is called Automatic Block Signalling.

Remote control

Because trains travel so fast, it would be easy for the driver of a high-speed train to miss a signal. For this reason many high-speed

FACT FILE

○ Most countries have Automatic Train Protection available, but some companies choose not to use it. It can make mistakes and hold up trains for no reason.

○ Look out for signals and warning signs at railroad stations and during train journeys.

The lights on the back wall of this control centre represent sections of the railrway track (blocks).

railways have no signals at all on the trackside. Instead, a control centre gathers information about the speed and position of all the trains in its area. This information is then sent to the trains by pulses of electricity through the rails. Computers in each train work out the distance to the train in front and the right speed to run at so that there is always enough room to stop if there is a problem. Instructions are shown on screens in the driver's cab. This type of system is called Continuous Cab Signalling, or CCS.

SIGNALING

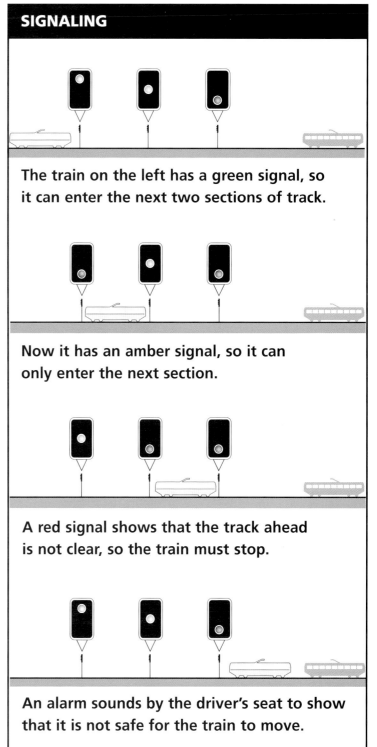

The train on the left has a green signal, so it can enter the next two sections of track.

Now it has an amber signal, so it can only enter the next section.

A red signal shows that the track ahead is not clear, so the train must stop.

An alarm sounds by the driver's seat to show that it is not safe for the train to move.

If the train goes faster than the speed limit, an alarm sounds, warning the driver to slow down. If the driver ignores the alarm, the train's computer takes over, cutting the power and turning on the brakes. This safety system is called Automatic Train Protection, or ATP.

This signal has turned red because a train has just passed it. The next train must stop.

Cutting through the air

Trains that are designed to travel at slow speeds often have a square, flat nose that makes them easier to join to other trains. They also have lots of boxes and equipment hanging underneath them, and there are big gaps between all the carriages.

When slow trains begin to move quickly, air starts to build up in front of them. The air begins to swirl around in circles before it is eventually swept back along the train as a twisting, turning mass. The air goes into the gaps between carriages and around the equipment under the train. In some places air even flows back toward the front of the train for a short time. A lot of the train's energy is wasted on moving the air.

A high-speed train has a very different shape. Its pointed nose moves through the air cleanly, disturbing it as little as possible. The air flows smoothly over the front of the train

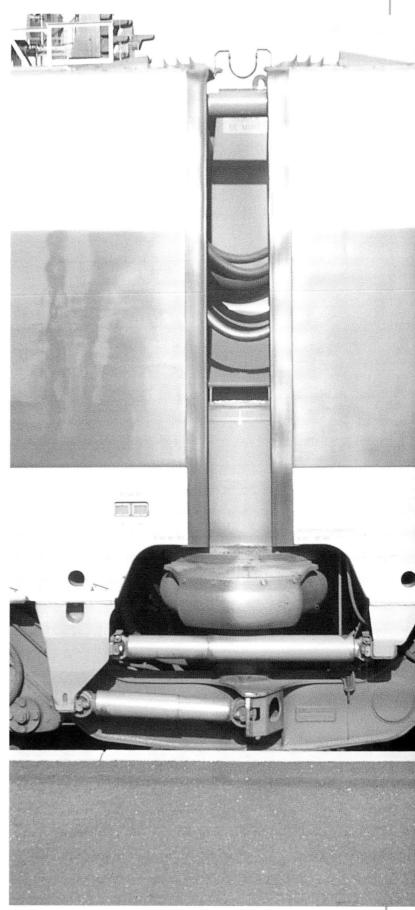

and back along its sides without swirling around too much. The underneath of the train is also made smooth so that the air flows in as straight a line as possible from the front of the train to the back.

The spaces between the carriages are kept very small so that air does not flow into the gaps, swirl around, and make the train travel slower and less efficiently.

Smooth running

Trains and other things that are shaped to move smoothly through the air like this are said to be streamlined. Streamlined trains are quieter because the air around them is much calmer. They are also cheaper to run because they don't waste a lot of energy just moving air around. Aeroplanes, rockets, and most modern cars are designed to cut easily through the air as well.

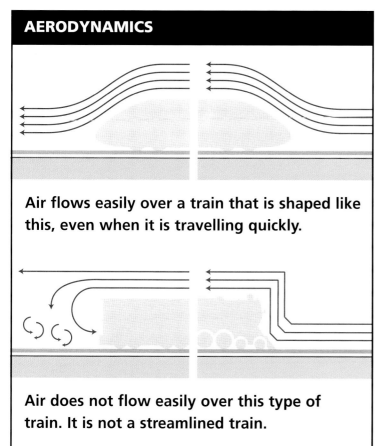

AERODYNAMICS

Air flows easily over a train that is shaped like this, even when it is travelling quickly.

Air does not flow easily over this type of train. It is not a streamlined train.

The space between these carriages is very small, so very little air can get caught up in the gap.

Full stop

High-speed trains travel very fast, so they need to have very good braking systems to slow them down quickly. There are many types of brake on high-speed trains, and they are all used at different speeds.

When the driver needs to slow down from a high speed, the first type of brake that is used is called a regenerative brake. It is a way of using the electric motors that usually drive the wheels as brakes.

Normally electricity flows through the motors to make them turn so that they drive the train. When the motors are used as brakes, the electricity is turned off.

The motors, attached to the wheels of the train, keep on turning—the wheels are now turning the motors, not the other way round.

When the motors are turned by the train's wheels, they generate electricity. This electricity flows up through the pantograph, into the catenary and helps power other trains along the line. Regenerative braking is a great way of saving energy because the

Wheel   Brake pads   Steel disk   Axle

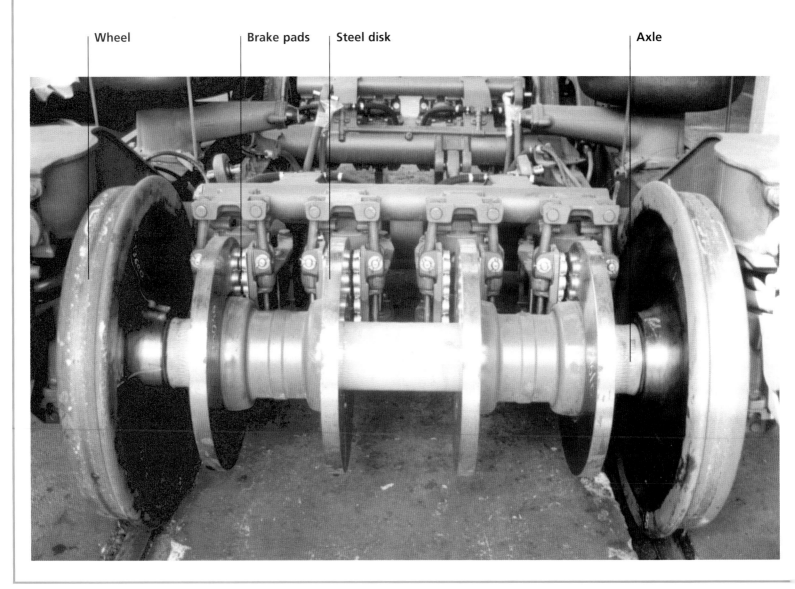

moving energy of the train is changed into electricity to use elsewhere.

Extra brakes

The second type of brake on a high-speed train is called a disk brake. A disk brake is quite a simple thing. A disk, made of steel, is fastened to the wheel. Around the disk there is a clamp called a calliper that has pads made of special material on either side of it. The disk and the pads can get very hot.

When the driver turns on the brake, the calliper squeezes the disk. It is a bit like the way a bicycle brake works by pinching the wheel between two blocks. It is the same type of brake that is found on most cars and motorbikes. The energy of the moving train is

The brakes are located on the wheels of each bogie but are controlled from the driver's cab.

turned into heat energy by the disk brake. The third type of brake is called a tread brake. The tread brake is only used when a train is moving at a very low speed. A tread brake is a band that fits around the outside of the train wheels just over the part of the wheel that runs on the track. When it is not being used, it sits just a fraction of an inch away from the wheel. When it is turned on, it grips the wheel. The energy of the moving train is turned into heat energy by the tread brake. Tread brakes have two uses: they help stop the train, and they also clean dirt off the wheels at the same time.

On the tracks

Many high-speed railways, like the TGV in France and the Acela Express in the United States, have tracks that are very like the ones used for slower trains. Often high-speed trains share some lengths of track with normal trains.

Once engineers have decided the best route for the line, the first stage is to level off the ground with construction machines. Next, a thick layer of gravel called ballast is laid over the ground. The ballast helps cushion the load of the trains as they move over the track. Concrete blocks called

sleepers or ties are laid on top of the ballast a few feet apart. Finally, the track is fastened on to the top of the sleepers using strong metal clips. Rubber pads are used under the clips

This track-laying machine runs on special wide rails that are taken away when the job is done.

to avoid putting too much stress on the concrete. Railway track is made from long lengths of steel. They are brought along the part of the track that has already been laid, carried on the top of special track-laying trucks. The lengths of track are joined together by welding. Welding makes the steel rails so hot that they melt and fuse together.

Special tracks

When a railway is built, the track is usually banked around corners. This means that trains taking the corner at high speed will lean into the turn, making the corner more comfortable for the passengers. High-speed trains need a track that is as straight as possible. When the track has to pass through areas with many mountains or rivers, a lot of expensive tunnelling, digging, and bridge building has to be done.

The Joetsu line in Japan has so many bridges, elevated sections (parts of the line that are held above the ground on concrete legs), and tunnels that only 1 percent of the line actually runs on the ground.

Once the track has been built, special trains run along it to keep it working well.

The track on this bridge is used by both high-speed trains and normal trains.

Weedkiller trains spray the ballast under the track so that plants cannot grow around the rails. Special recorders are used to test that the rails and ballast have not moved out of position. These track recorders measure any movement up and down or side to side as the train that carries them moves along the track. If any faults are found, a team of workers is sent to the problem area to fix it.

LAYING HIGH-SPEED TRACK

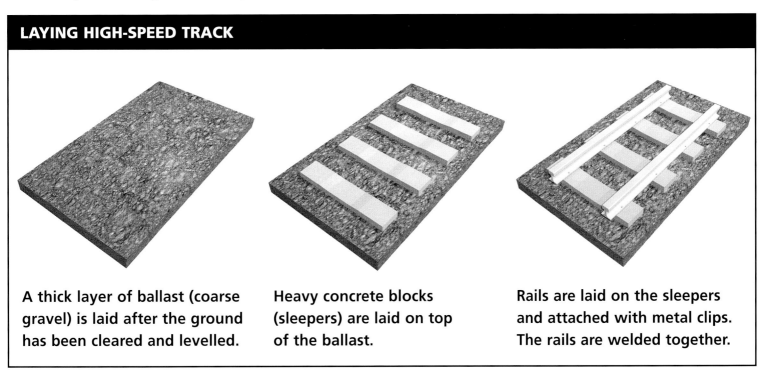

A thick layer of ballast (coarse gravel) is laid after the ground has been cleared and levelled.

Heavy concrete blocks (sleepers) are laid on top of the ballast.

Rails are laid on the sleepers and attached with metal clips. The rails are welded together.

Suspension

All trains have suspension systems with springs between the wheels and the rest of the train. The suspension gives a smooth ride for passengers and, more importantly, stops the train wheels from bouncing off the track as they pass over points and bumps.

This Swedish train tilts as it travels around corners. That enables it to travel even faster.

Many trains use springs made from coiled metal. When a wheel hits a bump in the track, it pushes up against the spring, which gets squashed. The spring always wants to go back to its original shape, so it pushes back against the wheel. The wheel is kept on the track. Because of the suspension it is just the wheel and the spring that move—not the whole carriage.

If just one spring was used for each wheel, it would bounce up and down lots of times whenever it hit a bump. To stop this from happening, a damper is attached to each wheel. The damper is designed to bounce at a different speed to absorb the vibration energy to produce a less bouncy ride.

FORCING AIR

Blow into the end of a bicycle pump, and see how the handle of the pump is forced out. This is how oil is forced into a ram when a train tilts.

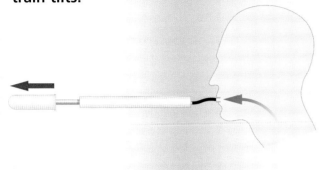

Many modern high-speed trains do not have steel springs. Instead, they use air suspension. Thick rubber bags filled with air take the place of the coil springs. Air suspension is lighter than metal springs and gives passengers a more comfortable ride. Some trains use both types of spring.

Some countries have so many hills that it is almost impossible for people to construct straight, fast railways. But even in the most hilly places trains can go more quickly if they lean over as they take corners. Most tilting trains work like this. As the train reaches a curve, sensors in each carriage send information to a computer. It works out how tight the curve is and sends a command to the tilting machinery of the carriage. Oil is forced into tubes called rams that tilt the carriage over to the side.

Without tilting carriages, passengers taking a corner at high speed would get thrown to one side and would not be very comfortable. With tilting, high-speed cornering feels quite safe.

TILTING TRAINS

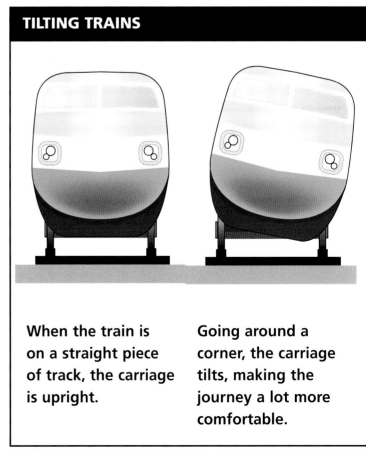

When the train is on a straight piece of track, the carriage is upright.

Going around a corner, the carriage tilts, making the journey a lot more comfortable.

Through and over

Sometimes the area that a railway needs to pass through is too steep or hilly for normal track. Maybe the track needs to cross a river or canyon. In these cases tunnels or bridges will have to be constructed.

Deep tunnels are dug using giant boring machines. At the front of the boring machine there is a circle of teeth that slowly turns, eating away at the rock. As the boring machine inches forward, the tunnel is lined with ready-made concrete slabs to give it extra strength. Sometimes when the tunnel has to pass through hard rock, the boring machine can move very slowly indeed. Even in the fairly soft chalk of the Channel Tunnel between France and England the boring machines took over a month to cover every mile (1.6km).

Tunnels are usually dug from both ends at the same time, so it is very important that the two ends meet properly in the middle. To make sure that they do, a laser beam is used. Laser light travels a long way and always travels in a straight line. Once the tunnel builders have worked out the right direction for the tunnel, the laser is used to point the way. The people working the boring machines just have to make sure that the laser is always shining on the middle of their machine.

Some shallow tunnels are built in a very different way. First, a deep trench is dug in the ground. Then, the trench is lined with concrete to make it strong. Next, the top of the trench is given a concrete roof, and the railway tracks are laid along the bottom. Finally, the top of the roof is covered with

A train crosses the Fraser River in New Westminster, Canada, using a cable-stay bridge.

soil so that it will blend in with the rest of the countryside. This way of building a tunnel is called cut-and-cover.

Bridges

Railways have always needed bridges to get them over rivers and valleys. The earliest bridges used pillars of stone and wood to support the track. Later, iron or steel girders were used, often in a complicated spider's web pattern called a truss. Many of these old bridges are still in use today.

A cable-stay bridge is often used for railways. To build this type of bridge, first a tower is built to support the weight of the bridge. Cables are then fastened between the tower and the platform that will carry the track. The platform is added to the bridge in stages, working in both directions at the same time. For longer bridges more than one tower is used.

These earthmoving machines are digging out a tunnel under Hong Kong Island.

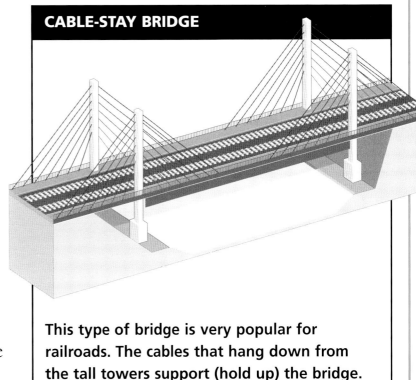

CABLE-STAY BRIDGE

This type of bridge is very popular for railroads. The cables that hang down from the tall towers support (hold up) the bridge.

The future

The Japanese bullet train was the first commercial high-speed train. This is the newest Shinkansen— it looks more like a rocket than a train!

High-speed trains running on metal rails will be used for many years to come. New versions will travel even faster, and some will even join together and split apart again on the move—getting people where they want to go as quickly as possible. But other types of train might one day take over.

One type of train that might be used in the future is called a MagLev. MagLev is short for MAGnetic LEVitation (lifted by magnets). MagLev trains do not touch their track as they move along. They do away with the noise and bumps of wheels running on a track by floating along on a magnetic field.

Magnets have two ends called poles. One is called the north pole, and the other is the south pole. If you take two magnets and try to push them together with north pole facing

north pole or south facing south, you will find it impossible—they just push themselves apart again. A MagLev train uses magnets in the same way.

Very strong electromagnets (*see* page 12) are put under the train. More electromagnets are put in the track. When electricity flows through the electromagnets, they push each other apart (repel) and lift the MagLev train into the air by a few inches.

Careful control of the electromagnets makes the train move along the track or stop. The only wheels on the MagLev train are used as it drops back onto the track when the electricity is turned off. Experimental MagLev trains have been built for many years, but up to now the longest MagLev in use is less than 19 miles (31km) long, connecting the city of Orlando to Disney World in Florida. However, in Japan people are experimenting with a new MagLev train system in Tokyo, and in Germany a MagLev system is due to start running in 2005.

Hovering

Another train of the future that would skim above the tracks is the hovertrain. Hovertrains use powerful fans to move air into the space between themselves and their track. The gap around the sides of the train is sealed with a rubber curtain called a skirt so that the air can not escape easily. The hovertrain is pushed along by a propeller like the propeller that drives an aeroplane. Hovertrains give a smooth ride, but experimental versions have, so far, been too noisy and expensive.

This MagLev train is being tested in Japan, the home of the high-speed train. MagLev trains could become popular one day.

FACT FILE

⚪ A 16-car Shinkansen (bullet train) can carry 1,300 passengers. It is 437 yards (400m) long.

⚪ A group of European companies is hoping to build the fastest rail service in the world in Spain. The trains will run between Madrid and Barcelona at speeds of up to 220 miles per hour (350km/h).

⚪ This web site contains paper models of high-speed trains for you to make: http://mercurio.iet.unipi.it/tgv/ papermodels.html

Glossary

ATP—stands for Automatic Train Protection. It is a safety system that stops the train if there is danger.

BALLAST—gravel bed that goes under the tracks of a railway.

BOGIE—a group of wheels under the train.

BORING MACHINE—a machine that cuts through the ground to make tunnels.

BULLET TRAIN—the popular name of the trains that run in Japan. In Japanese they are called Shinkansen.

DIESEL-ELECTRIC LOCOMOTIVE— a locomotive that uses a diesel engine to drive an electrical generator.

DISK BRAKE—a brake with a disk that is gripped by pads.

CATENARY—the overhead wires that carry electricity for trains.

ELECTROMAGNET—a magnet that only works when electricity flows through it.

ELECTRIC GENERATOR—a machine that turns the energy of movement into electrical energy.

GAS TURBINE—an engine that turns by using the energy of hot gas.

LOCOMOTIVE—a machine with motors and a driver's cab that pulls (or pushes) a train on railroad tracks.

MAGLEV—stands for MAGnetic LEVitation. A train that moves using powerful magnets.

PANTOGRAPH—the device on top of a train that touches the catenary and carries electricity to the motors.

POWER CAR—a part of a train with motors in it. Some high-speed trains have more than one power car.

REGENERATIVE BRAKE—a type of brake that uses the train's driving motors to slow it down.

SHINKANSEN—the Japanese high-speed railroad. It means "new main line."

SIGNALLING—a way of keeping trains a safe distance apart and giving information to the driver.

SLEEPERS—the beams that the track is attached to.

SUSPENSION—the springs that connect the body of the train to its wheels.

TGV—stands for Train à Grande Vitesse—the French for high-speed train.

TRACK RECORDER—a machine, carried on a train, that measures movements caused by faults on the track.

TREAD BRAKE—a brake that works by gripping the outside edge of the wheel.

WELDING—a way of joining pieces of metal together by heating them until they melt.

This is another version of the French TGV high-speed train. It travels mostly between Belgium and Germany, and is called the Thalys.

FURTHER INFORMATION

Books to read:
Trains by Jon Richards and Simon Tegg; Copper Beech Books, Brookfield, Conn; 1998.
Trains and Railroads by Sydney Woods and Sergio; Dorling Kindersley, New York, NY; 1998.

Web sites to look at:
http://www.acela.com
http://www.eurostar.com
http://www.japanrail.com
http://mercurio.iet.unipi.it
http://www.rtri.or.jp

Index

A
Acela Express 5
aerodynamics 18–19
air movements 8–9, 18–19
air suspension 25
aluminium 10, 11
Automatic Train Protection (ATP) 16, 17
axle 12, 20, 21

B
ballast 7, 22, 23
bogies 10–11
brakes, types 21
bridges 23, 26, 27
bullet trains 5, 7, 28

C
carriages 7, 10, 15
catenary 7, 13
chassis 10–11
computers 14, 17
construction 10–11
controls 14
curves 8, 23, 25

D
design 18–19
diesel motor 13
doors 15
driver's cab 14, 21

E
earthmovers 27
electric motors 12–13, 20
electromagnet 12, 13, 28
engine compartment 6
Eurostar 7, 31

G
geostationary orbit 24, 25

H
hovertrain 29

I
ICE (Inter-City Express) 5, 8–9

J
Japanese trains 5, 28, 29

M
MagLev train 28
magnets 28
materials 10–11

P
pantograph 7, 13
passengers 15
power 12–13
propeller 29
pylons 6, 13

R
rails 6, 22–23
remote control, signalling 16–17

S
safety 16, 17
seats 15
shape 18–19
signalling 16–17
sleepers 22, 23
springs 24
steel 10
stopping 20–21
suspension 6, 24–25

T
TGV (Train à Grand Vitesse) 5, 7, 31
tilting trains 24, 25
tracks 22–23
transmission 12
tunnels 8, 26–27

W
welding 10, 11, 23
wheels 7, 12, 20, 21
windows 11, 14
wires see *catenary*